THE YOM KIPPUR WAR

The Arab-Israeli Conflict of 1973

Written by Audrey Schul
In collaboration with Thomas Jacquemin
Translated by Carly Probert

History 50MINUTES.com

THE YOM KIPPUR WAR

KEY INFORMATION

- **When:** 6-26 October 1973
- **Where:** On the banks of the Suez Canal, Sinai Peninsula and Golan Heights (south west region of Syria) and the neighboring regions
- **Context:** The Arab-Israeli conflict
- **Belligerents:** Israel against Egypt and Syria, supported by Morocco, Saudi Arabia, Jordan and Iraq
- **Commanders and leaders:**
  - Golda Meir, Israeli Prime Minister (1898-1978)
  - Anwar Sadat, Egyptian President (1918-1981)
- **Outcome:** Israeli victory
- **Victims:**
  - Arab camp (Jordan, Iraq, Syria and Egypt): 9 500 dead and 19 850 wounded
  - Israeli camp: 3 020 dead and 8 135 wounded

INTRODUCTION

The Yom Kippur War was the fourth armed conflict between Israel and the Arab countries, namely Egypt and Syria, which would later result in the 1973 oil crisis.

On 6 October 1973, the day of Yom Kippur (Day of Atonement) for Jews, the Egyptians and Syrians carried out an armed attack in the Sinai Peninsula and the Golan Heights. First belonging to Egypt and Syria, these territories were conquered by Israel during the Six-Day War in 1967.

Although the Israeli fighting force was outnumbered, it managed to move gradually through Syria and cross the Suez Canal to finally reach the south and west of Egypt. A cease-fire was then declared by the United Nations Security Council in cooperation with the USSR and the United States in order to make room for negotiation. A peace plan was then agreed. However, the Israelis, not wishing to be interrupted in their advance, used the truce to continue their conquest, sparking further debates. New peace negotiations were then opened and led to the normalization of relations between Israel and Egypt. These negotiations were concluded in 1978 by the Camp David Accords, which stated that, in exchange for peace with Israel, Egypt would recover the Sinai Peninsula. The border between the two countries was opened once again.

POLITICAL AND SOCIAL CONTEXT

CRISIS IN THE MIDDLE EAST

Since the creation of the State of Israel in May 1948, relations between the country and the neighboring states in the Middle East were tense. The situation intensified even further during the 1960s. Indeed, during the Six-Day War in 1967, the Israeli army was very hostile towards Egypt, Syria and Jordan, from which it took several territories: the Gaza Strip and the Sinai Peninsula in Egypt, the Golan Heights in Syria and, finally, the West Bank and East Jerusalem in Jordan. Following these events, the Arab countries adopted the Khartoum Resolution in September 1967, which proposed:

- an ongoing struggle against Israel to regain the territories lost during the war;
- the use of Arab oil and its extraction as a diplomatic weapon;
- solidarity and military cooperation between the Arab countries;
- the defense of the rights of the Palestinian people;
- economic aid for Egypt and Jordan.

This became known as the "Three No's" resolution, because in its third paragraph, it turned against Israel and stated:

- no to peace with Israel;
- no to the recognition of Israel;
- no to negotiations with Israel.

A few months later, the UN Resolution 242 required the establishment of a lasting peace in the Middle East, the withdrawal of the Israeli troops from the occupied territories and the recognition of the Jewish state by the Arab countries. While on the Egyptian side, Anwar Sadat accepted the principles of peace, Israel refused to withdraw. Negotiations were blocked and they reached a state of status quo.

Seeking allies in the Middle East region in order to gain influence over what they considered to be a strategic territory, the Soviets decided to help the Egyptians and signed a treaty for peace and cooperation. Thus, the Soviet Union was committed to providing armaments to Egypt, in exchange for assurance of being able to retain its foothold in Egypt. At the same time, the Soviet leaders ensured the Egyptian's loyalty. However, for Egypt, things were different. Through this friendship treaty, the president was counting on increased help from his Soviet ally and asked for highly sophisticated weapons in order to defeat Israel and avenge the insult suffered in 1967. However, the USSR only sent defensive, not offensive weapons.

Meanwhile, in 1967, during important negotiations, the United States undertook to support Israel politically, economically and militarily in order to end the Middle East conflict. Thus, the United States showed its wish to recognize the Jewish state so that Resolution 242 would come into force. This would allow them to ensure that Israel could live in peace in the region, without compromising their economic interests.

PREPARATIONS FOR WAR

Of course, Egypt accepted the help of the Soviet Union because it was impossible to go into battle without receiving outside military assistance. However, in July 1972, relations between the two states declined, due to the will of the USSR to maintain the status quo in the Middle East. Consequently, Anwar Sadat considered the Soviet presence to be an obstacle to his freedom of action. In addition, the Soviet Union refused to provide certain types of weapons. These two reasons motivated his decision to remove the Soviet advisers from the territory. Even though talks resumed between Cairo and Moscow a few months later, the situation remained tense. Anwar Sadat remained intransigent and reiterated his call for offensive weapons. Afraid of undermining the spirit of international Détente, the Soviet leadership decided to hand over missiles, instead of the weapons requested. By doing this, without fulfilling the requirements of the Egyptian president, the USSR continued to militarily assist the country, while opposing military action.

However, Anwar Sadat gradually became aware that neither of the two great powers favored a change of power relations in the region and that they were likely to prefer a political solution, as opposed to a military one. This strongly contradicted his ambitions, as he wanted to form a large military force so that each Arab country close to the Jewish state could better defend itself. To this end, Egypt received financial assistance from Saudi Arabia, one of the leading states in the confrontation with Israel. Finally, Egypt received indirect assistance from Jordan, which was not openly committed, but participated in the offensive against the enemy through repeated threats, putting Israeli forces on permanent alert and preventing them from focusing on the Syrian and Egyptian fronts.

In Syria, the arrival of the new president Hafez al-Assad (1930-2000) in November 1970 caused discord in the relations between the two countries. However, the new Syrian president established military cooperation between his own country, Egypt, Iraq and, later, Jordan, in case a conflict broke out with Israel. The head of state proved uncompromising on foreign policy and rejected any attempts at peace with the Jewish state. He also received support from the USSR, prompting the Egyptian president to maintain good diplomatic relations with the country. But, given that the other Arab countries were conservatives who did not fully participate in the struggle against imperialism in the region, he refused the positions they adopted at the Khartoum conference, which strengthened his isolation in the Arab world.

Hafez al-Assad, 1996.

Despite the help that these countries brought to Egypt, the Arab states remained at a disadvantage compared to Israel, whose economic and social progress, as well as military development caused fear. The Arab states also wished to be heard on an international level and therefore required a significant political and economic force. However, they possessed a large amount of oil within their territories. They decided to use it by nationalizing the oil fields, making this material an important political weapon. Strengthened by this treasure, they decided to raise an embargo on the oil coming from the states that were opposed to the Arab claims and to use this as a means of pressure to force from the United States to recover the territories occupied by Israel since the Six-Day War. This was followed by a threat to reduce or even completely freeze oil production. Industrialized countries, such as the United States, Japan and Western Europe, depended on energy materials from Arab countries. Therefore, even if, politically, these countries had little interest in the Arab claims because they supported the Israeli policy, they became inevitably involved.

A SURPRISE ATTACK

When the Arab-Israeli conflict broke out, the international stage was seeing a period of lowering tensions. While in Washington, the Secretary of State Henry Kissinger (born in 1923) did not think that the war would take place, the Israeli leaders were more alert to the warning signs of a likely armed combat, such as the strengthening of control of roads leading to the Suez Canal, the warning from Anwar Sadat towards Yasser Arafat (Palestinian politician, 1929-2004) concerning an interruption of the cease-fire, the military preparations of the Arab forces located along the Suez Canal and in the Golan Heights, etc. Israeli intelligence deduced that an attack was likely, but no defense force was mobilized because Golda Meir, Prime Minister of the State of Israel, did not really believe them. Indeed, in the past, Egypt and Syria had mobilized their men repeatedly without ever declaring war on Israel. Moreover, the mobilization of the Israeli armed forces would be perceived by the Arabs as an act of aggression, not self-defense. Thus, by attacking, Israel would go against the spirit of Détente, which would not please the United States, whose weapon contribution was of the utmost importance.

At dawn on 6 October 1973, Ashraf Marwan (1945-2007), an Israeli spy – some believe he was linked to Egypt – warned the Jewish state that the Egyptian and Syrian attack was imminent: it would take place before sunset. He also delivered the order of battle and the canal passage plan developed by the Egyptians and the Syrians. Golda Meir immediately gathered her top military advisers and political leaders: Moshe Dayan (1915-1981), Yigal Allon (1918-1980) and Avraham Kidron. However, they struggled to reach an agreement over which fighting force to deploy. While General David Elazar (1925-1976) called for total mobilization – which included 200 000 men – and a preventive attack by the air force, Moshe Dayan opposed this and proposed a mobilization of the necessary defense forces. Hours later, the Council decided to mobilize the reserves on a large scale. But Golda Meir refused any preventive attack: the debate between Bayan and Elazar was thus settled. At 10:00am, the Prime Minister informed the United States that the beginning of the attack was planned for the afternoon, according to intelligence services, and that Israel would not launch hostilities.

COMMANDERS AND LEADERS

GOLDA MEIR, ISRAELI PRIME MINISTER

Golda Meir, March 1973.

Born in Kiev in 1898, Golda Meir was the first woman to become Prime Minister of Israel.

In 1948, she was among the figures who signed the Declaration of Independence of the State of Israel. After serving as an ambassador to the USSR and the Minister of Labor from 1949 to 1956, she became Foreign Minister in the cabinet of David Ben-Gurion (Israeli politician, 1886-1973). She asked for permission to change her last name (Mabovitch) into the Hebrew name Meir, meaning "illuminate".

In 1969, she became Prime Minister of Israel. Her term was marked by the Israeli victory and the extent of her conquests during the Six-Day War. Unfortunately, in 1973, the failure of Israeli intelligence to properly report the Arab attack during the Yom Kippur celebrations caused a major political upheaval. Indeed, while the agent Ashraf Marwan – it is still unclear today whether he was also working for Egypt – allegedly warned the director of the Mossad that an imminent attack was possible, the information was not directly transmitted. Feeling guilty for not triggering a preemptive attack, Golda Meir resigned on 11 April 1974, and Yitzhak Rabin (1922-1995) took over. Nicknamed the "grandmother of Israel", she died in Jerusalem in 1978.

ANWAR SADAT, EGYPTIAN STATESMAN

Anwar Sadat, January 1980.

Born in Egypt in 1918, Anwar Sadat was elected President of

the Arab Republic of Egypt in 1970. Before him, his predecessor, Gamal Abdel Nasser Hussein (1918-1970) had already intended to destroy the Jewish state. Wanting to achieve this aim, he set up a strategy to restore the Arab unity that had been undermined by the Six-Day War, in order to be stronger against Israel. To do this, Nasser Hussein decided to set up an Egyptian economic and military force. On his death, he was succeeded by Anwar Sadat. Unlike his predecessor, who led a defense policy centered on the Arab cause, the new Egyptian President primarily served the interests of Egypt as a nation.

In 1973, alongside Syria, he launched hostilities against Israel in an attempt to re-capture the Sinai, a territory which had been lost six years ago in the Six-Day War. Even though his country was defeated militarily and territorially at the end of the Yom Kippur War, for Anwar Sadat, the Arab honor lost during that year was restored anyway.

In 1977, he became the first Arab leader to visit Israel to meet with Prime Minister Menachem Begin (1913-1992), to find common ground. But many Arab authorities viewed the visit as a provocation. The following year, he participated in the signing of the Camp David Accords for peace in the Middle East: Arab unity against the Jewish state was thus broken. That same year, he received the Nobel Peace Prize. In 1979, the Camp David Accords were followed by the first peace treaty between Egypt and Israel.

On 6 October 1981, President Anwar Sadat was assassinated by members of the army belonging to the Egyptian jihad, who refused the agreement with Israel.

ANALYSIS OF THE WAR

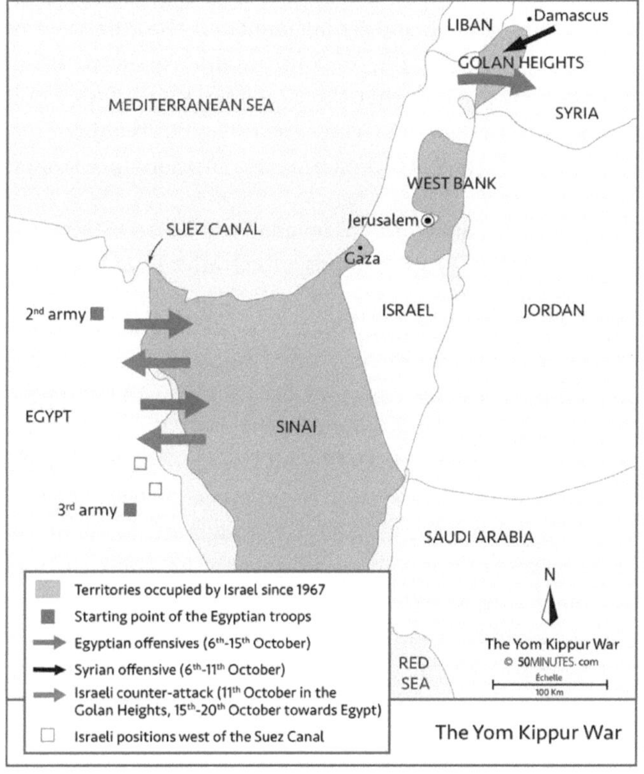

A WAR FOUGHT ON TWO FRONTS
(6-9 OCTOBER)

Arab armies (Egypt and Syria) launched the offensive on 6 October 1973, the day of Yom Kippur for Jews, taking advantage of the fact that the Israeli fighting forces would be fewer on that day because of their religious holiday. From the beginning, they attacked Israel on two separate fronts:

- in the north, Syrian forces invaded the Golan Heights;
- in the south, Egyptian forces entered the Sinai.

Therefore, two strategic areas were affected. The Golan territory was an area of vital importance for Israel because it provided access to Damascus, located only 48 kilometers from the cease-fire line established in 1967. By reaching the city, Israel could exclude the Syrian forces from the war. But the attack on the Golan Heights was preceded by an artillery barrage which began at 11:58am. Throughout the night, the Syrian forces continued their advance to the Golan Heights, their aim being to seize most of the territory to get control of the peaks of the mountains. On 7 October, Israel managed to progressively control the situation and in the evening, the Israeli army crossed the first line of Syrian defense and pushed back their armored vehicles. The Syrian air force was also undermined: the main airports were bombarded and Damascus was affected. Consequently, the Israeli response was costly for the Syrians. On 9 October, Israel managed to repel its enemy behind the cease-fire line of 1967.

While on the Golan front, the Syrian attack proved hasty,

that of the Egyptians was rather slow and assured. The Sinai offensive was calculated and prepared a long time in advance. Indeed, before the outbreak of the first clashes, Egypt had established an air defense system through the installation of surface-to-air missile (SAM) launchers and anti-air artillery to defend the SAM sites in the Suez Canal zone. Infrastructure was also built to launch and support an invasion beyond the canal. As for the Israelis, they built significant fortification lines, known as the Bar-Lev line, east of the canal. Once these lines were fortified, the Israel Defense Force no longer deployed any air defense weapons. Egypt therefore had in its possession a place on the first front line and highly sophisticated weapons, while Israel relied primarily on its fortification lines.

Egyptian forces use water cannons to cross Bar-Lev Line during the Yom Kippur War.

On 6 October, the Egyptian forces launched hostilities. Within hours, they arrived on the east bank and all positions in the first Israeli line were subject to significant attacks. On 7 and 8 October, Egypt continued its breakthrough in the Sinai. Israel then launched a series of attacks against them, with uncoordinated battalions that tried to destroy as many bridges placed by the Egyptian army on the canal as possible. However, the Egyptians arrived at the fortress of the second Bar-Lev line on 9 October and thus took control of the whole bank of the Suez Canal. Israel continued to defend itself, but did not launch a large-scale offensive.

At the announcement of the beginning of the conflict, the USSR and the United States did not show strong support for this. The resumption of hostilities in the Middle East called into question the spirit of Détente established between the two great powers. Therefore, none of them wanted to openly support an ally as the risk of extending the regional conflict to a more general confrontation was too large. This is why, after learning of the aid sent to Syria and Egypt by Moscow, Washington chose not to hold it against them, so that the situation was not embittered. Moreover, the United States decided to refuse any military aid to Israel and preserve peace.

THE ISRAELI COUNTER-ATTACK (10-13 OCTOBER)

After a period of hesitation, the Israeli leaders tried to control operations and, on 10 October, they chose to advance further on the northern front to reach Damascus, without necessarily wanting to occupy it. On the southern front, the Israeli government decided to prepare the forces for an attack across the canal, which was voluntarily delayed in order to allow the Egyptian army to disperse and weaken. Meanwhile, they focused their efforts on mobilizing their air forces, which was considered to be one of the best in the world. However, the Syrian and Egyptian SAM devices were more effective in combat than their own systems. Therefore, they did not succeed in destroying the Syrian and Egyptian air forces from the ground, and the Israelis were forced to fight in the air where they still retained a certain superiority. The strategic and economic targets, such as the city of Damascus, were the first affected. At the end of the day on 10 October, the Israelis controlled the airspace of Syria. Panic-stricken, it appealed to other Arab countries (Iraq, Kuwait and Morocco) to obtain military aid which arrived the next day. But, despite these reinforcements, Israel continued its progression.

On 11 October, Israel launched a general offensive and penetrated approximately 9.5 km into the Syrian heights. While the Syrian losses became more and more significant, the country was gradually weakening and hardly managed to push back its opponents. Aware of the danger posed by such a breakthrough, the Arab countries (Iraq, Morocco, Jordan and Saudi Arabia) were strengthening their military aid in order to protect Damascus and block the advance of the Israeli forces as soon as possible.

In the south, the situation was relatively calm in the Sinai. No major clash was reported. The Egyptians slowly consolidated their position along the strip they occupied east of the canal and, on 13 October, the Egyptian forces crossed the Suez Canal. This maneuver required the Israelis to move some of their fighting force to the southern front, so as to relieve the Syrian front.

After this second week of hostilities, the United States once again requested a cease-fire, which failed because the two great powers failed to agree on how to achieve definitive peace. Subsequently, U.S. political leaders decided to openly support Israel by providing military aid. Meanwhile, Soviet policy was more nuanced as it oscillated between compliance with its international interests (the agreement with the United States) and its supranational interests (keeping the Arabs as allies in the Middle East). On 12 October, negotiations resumed with the Soviet Union. While the Israeli government was in favor of the new proposed truce, diplomacy failed because President Anwar Sadat refused the proposal, unless Israel agreed to withdraw from all the territories it had occupied since 1967.

A DIPLOMATIC EVOLUTION (14-22 OCTOBER)

As of 14 October, the situation remained the same on the Golan Heights front as the Israeli offensive took place on the front of the Sinai. On 15 October, the Israelis continued to advance and reached the village of Sassa, located near Damascus. Facing them, the Syrians became increasingly weakened and suffered significant material losses: half of the air force and the majority of the armored vehicles were destroyed. But the Syrian army remained hopeful thanks to the different defense lines that blocked the road to Damascus, the density of the fortifications and the imposing artillery barrages, which slowed the Israeli progression. However, they could no longer launch a counter-attack because of the damage they had undergone. Their strategy paid off and the Israelis failed to destroy the last line of defense before Damascus.

On 14 October, Egypt launched a massive offensive by sending two armed divisions east of the Suez Canal. The plan was to carry out a frontal attack, with the aim of seizing certain territories to increase its flexibility in the east of the canal. The Egyptian Air Force participated in this first ground attack, but the operation ended in failure. Israel's victory in the Sinai demonstrated that Israel's military tactics were fully functional, as well as the fact that the Egyptian army was very vulnerable when it came out of its air defense envelope. The next day, the Israelis joined the channel and on 16 October, Israel extended its penetration:

the troops crossed the channel through their own pontoon bridge. Immediately, the Israeli forces moved northwards to destroy the anti-aircraft missile sites, in order to undermine the Egyptian defense. Meanwhile, Egypt was forced to recall the armed units east of the channel and stop the Israeli progress in the west. Once they had arrived in the west, the Israelis headed south to meet the ever weaker Egyptian forces.

On 22 October, when a cease-fire was called by the UN, the most advanced Israeli positions were blocking the road from Cairo to the city of Suez. Their armed forces were very effective and the Israelis acquired new military tactics over time. Noting the Israeli military successes achieved on Egyptian territory, the great powers began major di-plomatic maneuvers to establish a cease-fire as quickly as possible. The USSR and the United States did not want Israel to inflict another defeat upon the Arab countries, which would cause a considerable reduction in oil production as a sign of retaliation against the Israeli attitude. While the declarations of the two great powers were very ambiguous during the first ten days of the conflict, they suddenly clarified their positions on 16 October. The situation did not improve as, on 19 October, Israel was continuing to spread throughout Egypt, which was becoming increasingly vulne-rable. Therefore, the American and Soviet diplomats agreed on the need for an immediate cease-fire, as an escalation of violence was becoming more and more imminent. The Security Council was thus held on 22 October 1973 and established a new peace plan, known as Resolution 338.

THE BREAKING OF THE CEASE-FIRE (23-26 OCTOBER)

A few hours after the order of truce, the Israelis, who resented the fact that they had been interrupted when they were in a position of strength, resolved to improve their positions. On 23 October, they encircled the 3rd Egyptian army on the east bank of the canal and seized 20 000 men and 2 000 tanks. In response to this Israeli offensive, President Anwar Sadat appealed to the Soviet Union for help, which was granted, as the USSR did not want to lose its ally. In the United States, the Israeli attack was frowned upon as it undermined the negotiation process that had begun between the Americans and the Soviets. The US therefore exerted pressure on the Israeli government, so that it would respect the cease-fire. If Israel managed to destroy the 3rd Egyptian army, any US diplomacy in the Middle East would collapse.

When a new proposal for a cease-fire was presented by the US Secretary of State Henry Kissinger and the Soviet diplomat Anatoly Dobrynin Fedorovich (1919-2010) to Egypt, Anwar Sadat refused to sign the peace agreement, as the security of his 3rd army was not guaranteed by either of the two great powers. The Security Council then presented another peace plan that proposed to no longer entrust the surveillance mission to either of the great powers, but to an emergency UN force. On 24 October, a first group went into the field to monitor the troop movements. In the evening, the group met with the Israeli units and planted the UN flag in the ground, laying the border point between the two armies in doing so. On 25 October, a state of alert was launched by Henry Kissinger because Israeli forces were continuing to attack Egypt, despite the cease-fire, thus triggering the anger of the Soviets. The Soviets then decided to send troops to the Middle East to enforce the peace plan. Therefore, in order to prevent Soviet intervention in the Arab countries, US leaders threatened the USSR with the use of nuclear weapons if necessary. Faced with the firm attitude of Henry Kissinger and afraid of being dragged into a nuclear war, Moscow renounced its intervention, which in reality was nothing more than a signal addressed to the United States and to Israel calling for the cessation of hostilities. Very quickly, the two great powers decreed the end of hostilities in the Middle East and on 26 October, the attacks ceased on both sides of the Arab-Israeli borders. Calm was restored after 20 days of fighting, ending the Yom Kippur War. In total, the Israelis suffered the loss of 3 020 men and a further 8 135 wounded, while the Arab camp (Syria, Egypt, Jordan and Iraq) counted 9 500 dead and 19 850 wounded. However, although these hostilities were indeed terminated on the field, the crisis was far from settled.

REPERCUSSIONS OF THE WAR

FIRST NEGOTIATIONS

While the fighting had stopped, the 3rd Egyptian army was still stuck in the Sinai, which Egypt did not tolerate. It was therefore necessary to fix the situation. To do this, Henry Kissinger tried to harmonize the Israeli and Egyptian policies, and to calm the situation, the US Secretary of State called on the State of Israel to ensure supplies to the 3rd army and called on the Egyptian President to demonstrate patience and moderation. Appealing to the USSR would not have helped the situation, as the future of the crisis lay in the hands of the Israelis. At this point, it is important to emphasize that although negotiations were taking place between Moscow and Washington during the conflict, from the end of October they were now taking place in Jerusalem and the Arab capitals.

Despite emerging victorious from the conflict, the Israeli leaders proved to be quickly distraught by the situation in which they found themselves. Even if victory was theirs, they could see that the political and diplomatic situation had changed significantly:

- Relations between Israel and the Arab countries had turned. Indeed, Israel could no longer impose its policies, it must now negotiate.
- The involvement of the United States and the USSR increased the sense of urgency to adopt a more flexible policy towards the Arab countries.

- The defeat of the Arabs was relative. They lost militarily, but became politically assertive by using oil as a weapon.

The Israelis no longer had the confidence that they had gained after the Six-Day War. Although they knew that they had to negotiate with the Arab countries, they failed when it came to making concessions. Whereas Henry Kissinger tried to quickly obtain a peace agreement between Egypt and Israel, Golda Meir hesitated over the proposals to supply the 3rd army. The US Secretary of State then threatened to reduce the economic and political support given to the Israelis, and after lengthy discussions, the Israeli Prime Minister gave in. All that remained was to define the state that would monitor the free passage of the 3rd army. Israel decided to take the initiative, however Henry Kissinger had already suggested that Egypt take on the task or that the area fall under UN supervision. Therefore, the peace plan proposed by Henry Kissinger was still not suitable for Israel.

On the Egyptian side, Anwar Sadat was conciliatory and gave a glimpse of his intention to quickly reach an agreement. When Henry Kissinger told him that the Israelis had refused to give up control of the corridor, the Egyptian president, disappointed, finally accepted the conditions imposed by Israel. Satisfied with the conciliatory policy of Anwar Sadat, the US Secretary of State proposed to restore relations between Egypt and the United States. This agreement had a direct impact on Israel, which agreed a few days later to leave the control of the corridor, through which the 3rd army was supplied, to the UN forces. This shift reflected the fear felt by Israel of losing the Americans over the resumption of diplomatic relations that they held with Egypt. On 11 November 1973, the first agreement called the "Six Points" between Egypt and Israel was finally signed. It consisted of:

- a withdrawal from the occupied territories;
- the implementation of recognized borders;
- the creation of dematerialized areas;
- the recognition of borders by other Arab countries, but also by the United States and the Soviet Union;
- the recognition of the legitimate rights of the Palestinians;
- the recognition of the holy places in Jerusalem as being sacred to three religions.

The belligerents met at the 101st kilometer of the Cairo-Suez road to sign the six-point agreement, but negotiations between Egypt and the Arab countries were partial. The agreements that resulted were both due to the intense US diplomacy and the flexible policy of the Egyptian President Anwar Sadat. On 21 December 1973, new negotiations took place in Geneva, but they failed: at the beginning of 1974, the politics of the Middle East were once again compromised.

THE CAMP DAVID ACCORDS (1978)

The Yom Kippur War caused a shock for Israel. The invincibility of the army and the infallibility of the intelligence services were called into question. Whilst having all the necessary information specifying that an Arab attack was imminent, Israeli intelligence officials made interpretation errors, which were intensified by internal malfunctions, and therefore did not operate correctly. Furthermore, in operational terms, the Israelis did not respect the rules of the art of war, such as the economy of forces and the concentration of means, by using aviation and tanks in an irrational manner.

Following these errors, Golda Meir announced her resignation in April 1974. She was replaced by Yitzhak Rabin, whose government would be challenged by numerous scandals. Forced to call for another election, Menachem Begin became Prime Minister of Israel. However, these events slowed down the new peace negotiations. This is why the Egyptian president, who hoped to reach an agreement soon, decided to personally go to Israel. Through this decision, Anwar Sadat became the first Arab leader to recognize Israel's existence as a state. In 1978, US President Jimmy Carter (born in 1924) brought Anwar Sadat and Menachem Begin together for a summit at Camp David. Discussions lasted more than ten days and led to an Israeli-Egyptian peace treaty. However, the signing of the truce raised a considerable amount of discontent within the Arab community, which did not hesitate to exclude Egypt from the Arab League. In 1981, Anwar Sadat was assassinated by members of the army who disapproved of the peace agreement with Israel.

Jimmy Carter, Anwar Sadat and Menachem Begin during the signature of the Israeli-Egyptian peace treaty in Washington, 26 March 1979.

While the military victory lay with the Jewish state, the conflict provided the Arabs with a symbolic success. Using oil as a weapon and playing on the conflict between the two great powers, they were able to give a global character to this crisis and give new momentum to the Arab-Israeli struggle. Solidarity among the Arab countries gathered against Israel was finally found, which represented a great victory for them.

A CONFLICT AT THE FOREFRONT OF TECHNOLOGY

Due to the high-tech weaponry used, the Yom Kippur War remains the first high-intensity mechanized conflict since the end of World War II (1939-1945). Besides the fact that it demonstrated the importance of intelligence to counter a surprise attack, the Arab-Israeli conflict was also an opportunity to try out various weapons that had never been tested on the battlefield. This sophisticated technology had a great influence on the course of the conflict. Despite this, the importance of the human factor in the conduct of a battle was once again proven.

SUMMARY

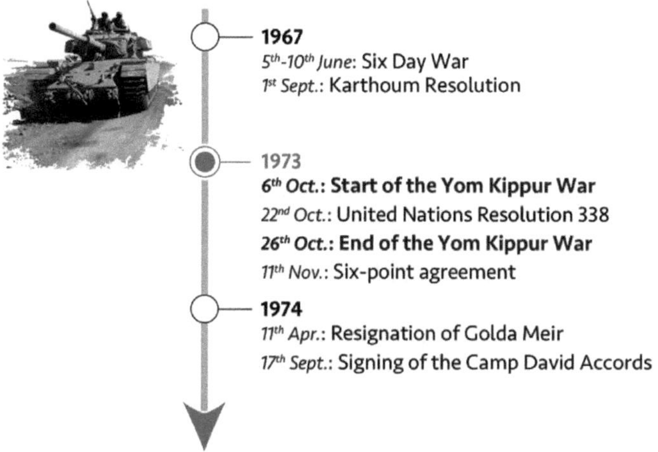

- Following the Israeli victory against Egypt, Syria and Jordan during the Six-Day War, the Khartoum Resolution was signed to define a common policy among the Arab countries.

- On 6 October 1973, the Arab armies attacked the Israelis on the day of Yom Kippur in the Sinai Peninsula and the Golan Heights, Syrian and Egyptian territories that had been occupied by Israel since the Six-Day War.

- On 9 October 1973, Israel managed to repel the Syrian attacks, but remained hesitant towards Egypt, which continued its breakthrough and now controlled the whole bank of the Suez Canal.

- The situation in the United States and the USSR was difficult: they did not want a direct confrontation that would jeopardize the process of Détente, but wanted to retain their respective areas of influence in the Middle East. The United States eventually encouraged Egypt to force Israel to cease fire, while the USSR provided some – but not all – of the weapons requested by the Arab countries.

- On 10 October 1973, a first attempt to establish a cease fire began, but amounted to nothing. The two great powers disagreed over how to achieve definitive peace. Two days later, new negotiations were set in motion. Although Israel agreed, the Egyptian president refused them unless Israel agreed to withdraw from all the territories it had occupied since 1967.
- On 14 October 1973, the Israeli army was victorious in the Sinai and reached the Suez Canal the following day.
- On 19 October 1973, when the Israeli advance was confirmed, the United States and the USSR agreed on the need for an immediate cease-fire, afraid that Israel would inflict another defeat upon the Arab countries, which would cause a considerable reduction in oil production.
- On 22 October 1973, the United Nations Security Council met and established a new peace plan: Resolution 338. The belligerents were ordered to cease all military activities in order to start negotiations for lasting peace.
- However, annoyed that their progression had been halted, the Israeli army broke the terms of the cease-fire and encircled the 3rd Egyptian army on the east bank of the canal. A new proposal for a cease-fire was then put on the table. But Anwar Sadat refused to sign the peace agreement as the security of his army was not guaranteed by the two great powers. The Security Council provided a solution by sending an emergency UN force into the field.

- On 26 October 1973, all fighting ceased on both sides of
  the Arab-Israeli borders. This marked the end of the Yom
  Kippur War.

FIND OUT MORE

BIBLIOGRAPHY

- Decker, A. and Nicolas, B. (1973) *Kilomètre 101. De la guerre du "Yom Kippour" à la Conférence de Genève.* Brussels: Édition des Archers.
- L'Encyclopédie Universalis (No date) *Kippour, Guerre du (Oct. 1973).* [Online]. [Accessed 8 December 2016]. Available from: <http://www.universalis.fr/encyclopedie/guerre-du-kippour/>
- L'Encyclopédie Universalis (No date) *Yom Kippūr ou Yom Kippour.* [Online]. [Accessed 8 December 2016]. Available from: <http://www.universalis.fr/encyclopedie/yom-kippur/>
- Atlas Historique du Monde (2005) *Guerre du Kippour.* Toulouse: Éditions Parragon.
- Heymans, C. (1982) *Le quatrième conflit israélo-arabe. La guerre du Kippour.* Unpulbished Master's thesis. Louvain-la-Neuve.
- Laqueur, W. (1974) *La vraie guerre du Kippour.* Paris: Calmann-Lévy.
- Michal, B. (1975) *Les guerres israélo-arabes.* Geneva: Éditions Famot.
- Michel, A. (1998) *Racines d'Israël. 1948 : une plongée dans 3000 ans d'histoire.* Paris: Autrement.
- Mirel, P. (1982) *L'Égypte des ruptures. L'ère Sadate, de Nasser à Moubarak,* Paris: Éditions Sindbad.
- Porat, B., Gueffen, J., Dan, U. et al. (1974) *Kippour.* Paris: Hachette.
- Razoux, P. (2004) *La guerre des Six Jours (5-10 juin 1967).*

Du mythe à la réalité. Paris: Economica.
- Razoux, P. (1999) *La guerre du Kippour d'octobre 1973*.
  Paris: Economica.

ADDITIONAL SOURCES

- Asher, D. (ed.) (2016) *Inside Israel's Northern Command: The Yom Kippur War on the Syrian Border*. Lexington: University Press of Kentucky.
- Herzog, C. (2010) *The War of Atonement: The Inside Story of the Yom Kippur War*. London: Greenhill Books.
- Meir, G. (1976) *My Life*. London: Futura Publications.
- Rabinovich, A. (2005) *Yom Kippur War*. New York: Random House.

ICONOGRAPHIC SOURCES

- Hafez al-Assad, 1996. Royalty-free reproduction picture.
- Golda Meir, March 1973. © Marion S. Trikosko.
- Anwar Sadat, January 1980. Royalty-free reproduction picture.
- Egyptian forces use water cannons to cross Bar-Lev Line during the Yom Kippur War. Photo from the book *Military Battles on the Egyptian Front*, by Gammal Hammad, Le Caire, Dār al-Shurūq, 2002. Royalty-free reproduction picture.
- Jimmy Carter, Anwar Sadat and Menachem Begin during the signature of the Israeli-Egyptian peace treaty in Washington, 26 March 1979. © Warren K. Leffler.

FILMS AND DOCUMENTARIES

- *Kippur.* (2000) [Film]. Amos Gitai. Dir. Israel: Canal+, Agav Hafakot.
- *Israel and the Arabs: Elusive Peace.* (2005) [Documentary]. Norma Percy. Dir. UK: Brook Lapping Productions.

ISHIKAWA DIAGRAM
Material Method Machine
Mother Nature Measure Men
Management & Marketing 50MINUTES.com
THE BATTLE OF AUSTERLITZ
ADAM SMITH